Maths

Age 8-9

Contents

Activities

Quick Tests

Paul Broadbent and Peter Patilla

Numbers to *1000*

The numbers between 100 and 999 all have **three digits**.

$$376 \rightarrow 300 + 70 + 6$$

hundreds tens ones

When you add or subtract 1, 10 or 100, the digits change.

$$376 + 1 = 377 \qquad 376 + 10 = 386 \qquad 376 + 100 = 476$$

1 Continue these number chains.

a 757 → (+ 1) → ☐ → (+ 1) → ☐ → (+ 1) → ☐

b 628 → (– 10) → ☐ → (– 10) → ☐ → (– 10) → ☐

c 496 → (+ 10) → ☐ → (+ 10) → ☐ → (+ 10) → ☐

d 641 → (+ 1000) → ☐ → (+ 1000) → ☐ → (+ 1000) → ☐

e 385 → (– 100) → ☐ → (– 100) → ☐ → (– 100) → ☐

f 9030 → (– 1000) → ☐ → (– 1000) → ☐ → (– 1000) → ☐

2 Complete this number puzzle.

Across

1 Seven hundred and forty-three

5 Nine hundred and twenty

6 Eight thousand and seventy-four

Down

2 Four hundred and nine

3 Three hundred and fifty-one

4 Six hundred and eight

7 Nine thousand, six hundred and four

Number sequences

A sequence is usually a list of **numbers in a pattern**.

Look at the difference between each number to spot the rule for the pattern.

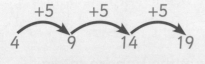

4   9   14   19

The rule is +5

23   20   17   14

The rule is −3

1 Write the missing numbers in these sequences. What is the rule for each of them?

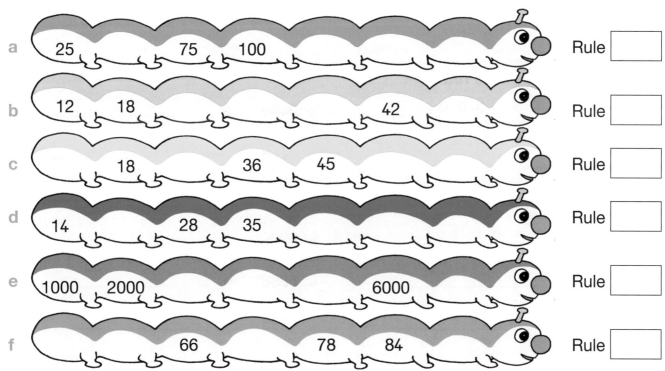

a   25   75   100   Rule [   ]

b   12   18   42   Rule [   ]

c   18   36   45   Rule [   ]

d   14   28   35   Rule [   ]

e   1000 2000   6000   Rule [   ]

f   66   78   84   Rule [   ]

2 Negative numbers go back past zero. Write the missing numbers on these number lines.

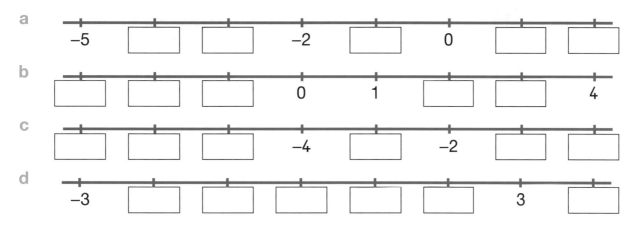

a   −5 [   ] [   ] −2 [   ] 0 [   ] [   ]

b   [   ] [   ] [   ] 0   1 [   ] [   ] 4

c   [   ] [   ] −4 [   ] −2 [   ] [   ]

d   −3 [   ] [   ] [   ] [   ] [   ] 3 [   ]

3

Place value

4-digit numbers are made from **thousands**, **hundreds**, **tens** and **ones**.

Rounding to the nearest 100

653 rounds **up** to 700

439 rounds **down** to 400

Look at the **tens** digit.

- If it is 5 or more, round up to the next hundred.

- If it is less than 5, the hundreds digit stays the same.

Rounding to the nearest 1000

4621 rounds **up** to 5000

3107 rounds **down** to 3000

Look at the **hundreds** digit.

- If it is 5 or more, round up to the next thousand.

- If it is less than 5, the thousands digit stays the same.

---

1 Write the value of the red digit.

a 3450 → _____5 tens_____

b 6795 → _____

c 4008 → _____

d 9217 → _____

e 3169 → _____

f 5291 → _____

g 9469 → _____

h 4778 → _____

i 7432 → _____

j 2984 → _____

k 8898 → _____

l 4793 → _____

2 Round each number to the nearest 100 or 1000.

a 385

b 790

c 368

d 412

e 545

f 4659

g 2910

h 3400

i 5070

j 8500

Addition

When you add numbers, decide whether to use a **mental method** or a **written method**.

Mental method

160 + 59

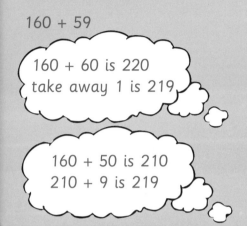

160 + 60 is 220
take away 1 is 219

160 + 50 is 210
210 + 9 is 219

Written method

4365 + 3718

$$
\begin{array}{r}
4365 \\
+\ 3718 \\
\hline
8083 \\
\end{array}
$$

¹   ¹

Start with the ones and add each column. Don't forget to 'carry over' any tens, hundreds or thousands.

---

1 Use the numbers from the grid to answer these.

a Which two numbers total 140? ☐ and ☐

b What is the sum of the two largest numbers? ☐

c What is the total of the three smallest numbers? ☐

d What is the sum of the four corner numbers? ☐

e Which two numbers add up to 210? ☐ and ☐

f What is the sum of the numbers in the top row? ☐

75	290	54
250	165	86
38	124	62

---

2 Use a written method to answer these.

a   5094
    + 3168
    _____

c   4816
    + 1247
    _____

e   £17.90
    + £28.54
    _____

g   £35.29
    + £13.46
    _____

b   3629
    + 8294
    _____

d   1498
    + 7527
    _____

f   £87.91
    + £48.14
    _____

h   £38.54
    + £27.86
    _____

2-D shapes

A **polygon** is any 2-D shape with straight sides.

Count the number of sides to help name different polygons.

triangle   pentagon   heptagon   nonagon

A regular polygon has equal sides and equal angles.

quadrilateral   hexagon   octagon   decagon

---

1 Name each shape. Tick the regular polygons.

a   ☐ _____

b   ☐ _____

c   ☐ _____

d   ☐ _____

e   ☐ _____

f   ☐ _____

g   ☐ _____

h   ☐ _____

i   ☐ _____

j   ☐ _____

k   ☐ _____

l   ☐ _____

---

2 Use a pencil and a ruler to draw each of the named shapes accurately.
One line in each shape is already drawn.

a

rectangle

b

hexagon

c

octagon

d

right-angled triangle

e

square

f

equilateral triangle

g

regular pentagon

h

heptagon

Ordering numbers

To help work out the order of numbers, write them in a list. Make sure you line up the ones column.

Look at the numbers. Compare the **thousands**, then the **hundreds**, then the **tens** and finally the **ones** column.

729
792
7209
7290

1 Write these in order, starting with the smallest.

a
£1090
£1900
£958
£2850
£2589

b
3755 km
965 km
3095 km
3520 km
2830 km

c
2046 g
2460 g
2604 g
1599 g
1995 g

d
7025 ml
4599 ml
7529 ml
4600 ml
7028 ml

_____ _____ _____ _____

_____ _____ _____ _____

_____ _____ _____ _____

_____ _____ _____ _____

_____ _____ _____ _____

2 Use the digits

Make as many different 4-digit numbers as you can. Write them in order, starting with the smallest.

Time of day

There are 60 minutes in an hour and 24 hours in a day.

am stands for **ante meridiem** and means **before midday**.

pm stands for **post meridiem** and means **after midday**.

5.35am

35 minutes past 5 in the morning

7.15pm

15 minutes past 7 in the evening

1 Draw the hands on the clock or write the digital time for each start and finish time.

Start   **Finish**

a  Mark goes swimming at 10.15am. He gets home $1\frac{1}{2}$ hours later.

b Start clock A train leaves London at 6.20pm. It arrives at Leeds 2 hours 20 minutes later.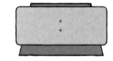

c  Becky goes shopping at 11.10am. She finishes 3 hours 45 minutes later.

d Start clock A football match starts at 1.45pm. It finishes 90 minutes later.

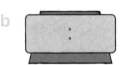

2 This timetable shows the times of buses. If you are at a bus stop at these times, how long will you have to wait?

BUS TIMETABLE

7.40am	8.15am	9.20am	10.50am	11.40am
2.10pm	4.30pm	5.10pm	6.30pm	8.00pm

a 9.05am = _____ minutes   d 10.35am = _____ minutes

b 11.15am = _____ minutes   e 7.40pm = _____ minutes

c 5.05pm = _____ minutes   f 4.45pm = _____ minutes

Fractions

There are **two numbers** that show a fraction:

$$\frac{2 \rightarrow \text{numerator}}{3 \rightarrow \text{denominator}}$$

The **denominator** shows the number of equal parts.

The **numerator** shows how many of the equal parts are used.

Equivalent fractions are worth the same.

$$\frac{2}{3} = \frac{4}{6} = \frac{8}{12}$$

We usually write fractions using the smallest possible denominator.

1 Complete the equivalent fractions. In a-d use the diagram to help you complete the first fraction.

a
$$\frac{\square}{10} = \frac{\square}{5}$$

b
$$\frac{\square}{12} = \frac{\square}{3}$$

c
$$\frac{\square}{8} = \frac{\square}{4}$$

d
$$\frac{\square}{15} = \frac{\square}{5}$$

e $\dfrac{8}{12} = \dfrac{\square}{3}$

f $\dfrac{\square}{18} = \dfrac{1}{2}$

g $\dfrac{4}{20} = \dfrac{1}{\square}$

h $\dfrac{20}{50} = \dfrac{2}{\square}$

i $\dfrac{\square}{20} = \dfrac{9}{10}$

j $\dfrac{18}{24} = \dfrac{3}{\square}$

2 Write these fractions in order, starting with the smallest. Use the wall to help you.

$\dfrac{3}{5}$ $\dfrac{9}{10}$ $\dfrac{1}{4}$

$\dfrac{3}{4}$ $\dfrac{2}{3}$

$\dfrac{1}{10}$

$\dfrac{1}{2}$ $\dfrac{2}{10}$

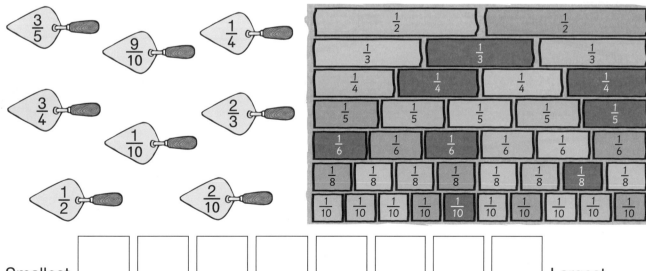

Smallest ☐ ☐ ☐ ☐ ☐ ☐ ☐ ☐ Largest

9

Measuring length

Look at these lengths.

10 millimetres (mm)	= 1 centimetre (cm)
100 cm	= 1 metre (m)
1000 m	= 1 kilometre (km)

Short lengths can be measured in millimetres.

Long distances can be measured in kilometres.

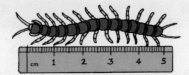

PARIS 380km

1 Write these equivalent lengths.

a $3\frac{1}{2}$ km = ◻ m

b 40 mm = ◻ cm

c 150 cm = ◻ m

d 8 cm = ◻ mm

e $\frac{1}{4}$ m = ◻ cm

f 6500 m = ◻ km

g 22 cm = ◻ mm

h 18 km = ◻ m

i $4\frac{3}{4}$ m = ◻ cm

j 65 mm = ◻ cm

2 Use a ruler to measure these lines in millimetres.

a ◻ mm

b ◻ mm

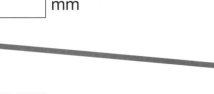

c ◻ mm

d ◻ mm

e ◻ mm

Multiplication and division

Multiplication and division are **linked**.

$6 \times 5 = 30$ If you know this, there are three other facts you also know.

$5 \times 6 = 30$
$30 \div 5 = 6$
$30 \div 6 = 5$

The three numbers 6, 5 and 30 are sometimes called a trio.

1 Write four facts for each of these trios.

a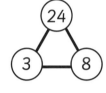

☐ × ☐ = ☐

☐ × ☐ = ☐

☐ ÷ ☐ = ☐

☐ ÷ ☐ = ☐

b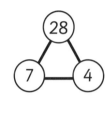

☐ × ☐ = ☐

☐ × ☐ = ☐

☐ ÷ ☐ = ☐

☐ ÷ ☐ = ☐

Write the missing numbers.

c ☐ × 6 = 36

d ☐ ÷ 3 = 7

e 54 ÷ ☐ = 9

f 4 × ☐ = 48

g 8 × ☐ = 32

h 45 ÷ ☐ = 9

i ☐ ÷ 7 = 11

j ☐ × 6 = 48

2 If a number cannot be divided exactly, it leaves a remainder. Draw a line to join each division to its matching remainder.

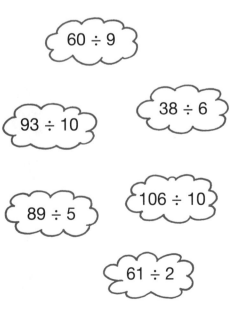

60 ÷ 9

80 ÷ 3

37 ÷ 3

53 ÷ 6

38 ÷ 6

93 ÷ 10

48 ÷ 5

89 ÷ 5

106 ÷ 10

46 ÷ 6

61 ÷ 2

65 ÷ 6

Comparing numbers

The symbols > and < are used to compare numbers.

<

means 'is less than'

729 < 750

729 is less than 750

>

means 'is greater than'

2500 > 2100

2500 is greater than 2100

1 Write the signs > or < for each pair of numbers.

a   455 ☐   396   g   3750 ☐   3079

b   817 ☐   870   h   6002 ☐   6010

c   958 ☐   936   i   5299 ☐   5300

d   1904 ☐   2301   j   7451 ☐   7415

e   1850 ☐   1508   k   5306 ☐   5311

f   2001 ☐   1998   l   9038 ☐   9009

2 Write the numbers that could go in each middle box.

a   4169 > ☐ > 4164   _____ _____ _____

b   3838 < ☐ < 3842   _____ _____ _____

c   9002 > ☐ > 8996   _____ _____ _____

d   4421 < ☐ < 4426   _____ _____ _____

e   7082 > ☐ > 7076   _____ _____ _____

3-D shapes

A **polyhedron** is a 3-D shape with flat faces.

A cube is a polyhedron. It has:

- 8 vertices (corners)
- 12 edges
- 6 faces.

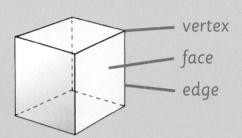

1 Name each shape. Choose the correct word from the box.

cylinder
cone
cube
pyramid
sphere
cuboid

a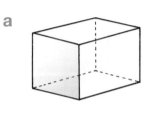

c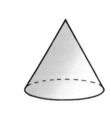

e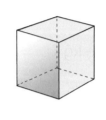

_____   _____   _____

b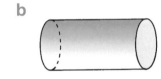

d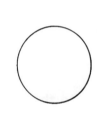

f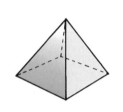

_____   _____   _____

2 Write how many faces, edges and vertices each shape has.

	faces	edges	vertices
a 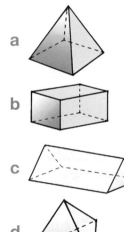	_____	_____	_____
b	_____	_____	_____
c	_____	_____	_____
d	_____	_____	_____

Measuring mass

Kilograms (kg) and **grams** (g) are some of the units we use to measure the weight or mass of an object.

$$1000\ g = 1\ kg \qquad 250\ g = \tfrac{1}{4}\ kg$$
$$500\ g = \tfrac{1}{2}\ kg \qquad 750\ g = \tfrac{3}{4}\ kg$$

1 Write these equivalent units.

a 2000 g = [ ] kg

b $1\tfrac{1}{2}$ kg = [ ] g

c 5500 g = [ ] kg

d 1250 g = [ ] kg

e 7 kg = [ ] g

f $3\tfrac{1}{4}$ kg = [ ] g

g 10 kg = [ ] g

h 6750 g = [ ] kg

i $2\tfrac{1}{2}$ kg = [ ] g

j $4\tfrac{3}{4}$ kg = [ ] g

k 9500 g = [ ] kg

l $1\tfrac{3}{4}$ kg = [ ] g

2 Look at these scales. Write the mass shown in kilograms.

a

_____

b

_____

c

_____

Write the mass shown in grams.

d
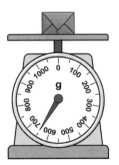
_____

e

_____

f
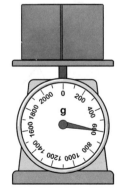
_____

Subtraction

If you cannot **subtract** numbers mentally, use a written method. Look at these two methods for 734 − 278.

Number line method

2 + 20 + 434 = 456

278 onto 280 is 2. 280 onto 300 is 20. 300 onto 734 is 434.

Column method

$$
\begin{array}{r}
6\,{}^{12}\!7\!{}^{1}\!3\!4 \\
-\ 278 \\
\hline
456
\end{array}
$$

- Start with the ones column, taking away the bottom number from the top.
- If the top number is smaller than the bottom, exchange a ten or a hundred.

---

1 Choose a method to answer these.

a Find the difference between 184 and 367.   ▢

b What is 253 subtract 176?   ▢

c What is 852 take away 483?   ▢

d Decrease 813 by 125.   ▢

e Subtract 218 from 1186.   ▢

f What is the difference between 2084 and 2257?   ▢

g What is 1437 minus 1185?   ▢

h What number is 2425 less than 3812?   ▢

2 Write the digits 2 to 9 on small squares of paper. Arrange them on these squares as subtractions so you can answer these.

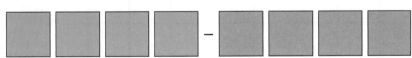

a What is the biggest answer you can make?   =   ▢

b What is the smallest answer you can make?   =   ▢

c Give an answer as near as possible to 2000.

Area

The area of a shape can be found by **counting squares on a grid**.

Count half squares for shapes with straight diagonal sides.

For irregular shapes, count the squares that are covered more than half.

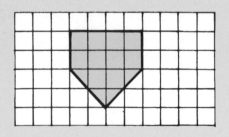

Area = 12 squares

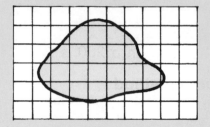

Area = approximately 19 squares

1 Work out the area of each shape.

a Area =
[ ] squares

b Area =
[ ] squares

c Area =
[ ] squares

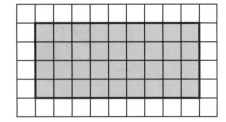

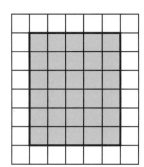

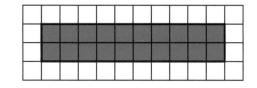

2 Draw two different rectangles with an area of 8 squares.

Written multiplication and division

Here are two methods of **multiplication**.

Here is a method of **division**.

Grid method

47 × 6

	6
40	240
7	42

282

Column method

47 × 6

```
    4 7
  ×   6
  -----
  2 8 2
  -----
    4
```

197 ÷ 6

```
        32 remainder 5
   6 | 197
      -180
       17
     -  12
        5
```

1 Use one of the methods above to answer these multiplication sums.

a 38 × 6 = ☐

b 54 × 7 = ☐

c 85 × 9 = ☐

d 64 × 8 = ☐

e 219 × 6 = ☐

f 324 × 7 = ☐

g 512 × 4 = ☐

h 284 × 5 = ☐

Working out

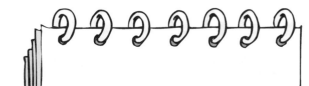

2 Answer these division problems.

a
```
4 | 7 5 6
```

b
```
7 | 9 1 4
```

c
```
5 | 9 0 7
```

d
```
8 | 6 4 5
```

Use the numbers in the box below to answer the following division problems.

| 691 | 438 | 602 | 358 | 696 |

e Which of the numbers in the box can be divided exactly by 7? ☐

f Which of these numbers has a remainder of 3 when divided by 8? ☐

g Which of these numbers is exactly divisible by 4? ☐

h Which of these numbers has an answer of 73 when divided by 6? ☐

i Which of these numbers has a remainder of 4 when divided by 6? ☐

Symmetry

A shape is symmetrical if both sides are exactly the same either side of a **mirror line**, like a reflection.

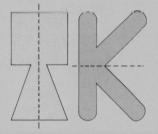

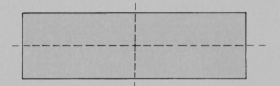

This rectangle has two lines of symmetry.

1 Draw the reflection of each of these.

a
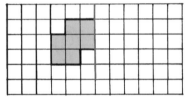

c
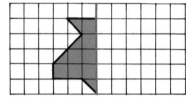

e

b
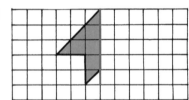

d

f
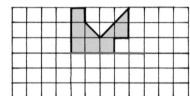

2 Draw lines of symmetry on these shapes. Write the number of lines of symmetry for each shape.

a

☐ lines of symmetry

c

☐ lines of symmetry

e

☐ lines of symmetry

b

☐ lines of symmetry

d

☐ lines of symmetry

Measuring capacity

Litres (l) and **millilitres** (ml) are some of the units we use to measure the capacity of liquids in containers.

1000 ml = 1 l   750 ml = $\frac{3}{4}$ l

250 ml = $\frac{1}{4}$ l   500 ml = $\frac{1}{2}$ l

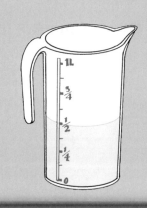

1 Write the equivalent units.

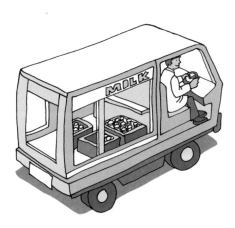

a 3000 ml = [ ] l

b 1$\frac{1}{2}$ l = [ ] ml

c 6 l = [ ] ml

d 2250 ml = [ ] l

e 1750 ml = [ ] l

f 10 l = [ ] ml

g 3$\frac{1}{2}$ l = [ ] ml

h 2000 ml = [ ] l

i 4500 ml = [ ] l

j 8$\frac{3}{4}$ l = [ ] ml

k 5750 ml = [ ] l

l 6$\frac{3}{4}$ l = [ ] ml

2 Write the capacity each jug shows in millilitres.

a

[ ] ml

c

[ ] ml

e

[ ] ml

g

[ ] ml

b

[ ] ml

d

[ ] ml

f

[ ] ml

h
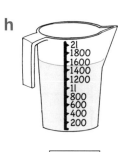
[ ] ml

Decimals

A **decimal point** is used to separate whole numbers from fractions.

$0.1 = \frac{1}{10}$

$0.5 = \frac{5}{10} = \frac{1}{2}$

$1.03 = 1\frac{3}{100}$

$4.76 = 4\frac{76}{100}$

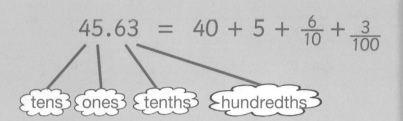

$$45.63 = 40 + 5 + \frac{6}{10} + \frac{3}{100}$$

tens ones tenths hundredths

---

1 Change these fractions to decimals.

a $\frac{3}{10}$ =

b $\frac{5}{10}$ =

c $\frac{2}{10}$ =

d $\frac{3}{4}$ =

e $\frac{17}{100}$ =

f $\frac{4}{10}$ =

g $\frac{41}{100}$ =

h $\frac{9}{10}$ =

i $\frac{65}{100}$ =

j $\frac{1}{2}$ =

k $\frac{59}{100}$ =

l $\frac{1}{4}$ =

---

2 Write the decimals on these number lines.

a

0   1

b

3   4

c

6.10   6.20

Reading bar charts

A **bar chart** shows information as a graph.

Read the scale and labels on the axes carefully.

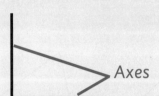
Axes

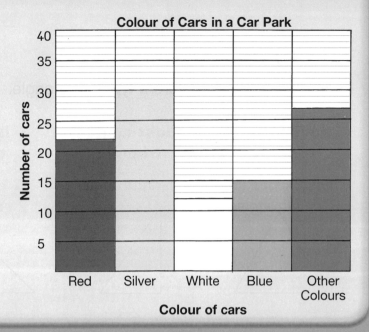

Colour of Cars in a Car Park

Number of cars

Colour of cars

Red   Silver   White   Blue   Other Colours

1 Look at the graph above and answer these.

a Which colour was the most common car colour in the car park? _____

b How many cars were white? _____

c How many more cars were red than white? _____

d Which colour had half the number of silver cars? _____

e Black was the most common 'Other colour', with $\frac{1}{3}$ of these cars black. How many cars in total were black? _____

f How many cars in total were in the car park? _____

2 This graph shows the number of cars visiting a car wash over five days.

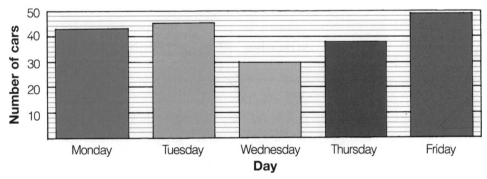

Number of cars

Monday   Tuesday   Wednesday   Thursday   Friday

Day

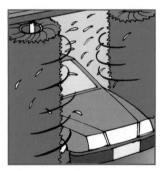

a How many cars visited the car wash on Tuesday? _____

b On which day did 38 cars visit the car wash? _____

c How many more cars visited on Friday than Monday? _____

d On which day did 15 fewer cars visit the car wash than on Tuesday? _____

Triangles

Learn the names of different types of triangle.

Equilateral triangle	Right-angled triangle	Isosceles triangle	Scalene triangle
3 equal sides and 3 equal angles	1 right angle	2 equal sides 2 equal angles	No sides the same length

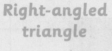 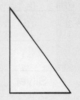 

1 Colour each triangle to match the key. Use a ruler to help you decide.

Key:

equilateral

isosceles

scalene

a b c 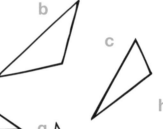 d

e  h

f  g  i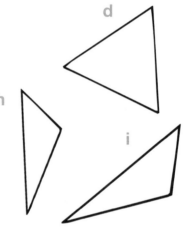

2 Write the letter of each triangle in the correct place on the Venn diagram.

a e

b f

c g

d  h

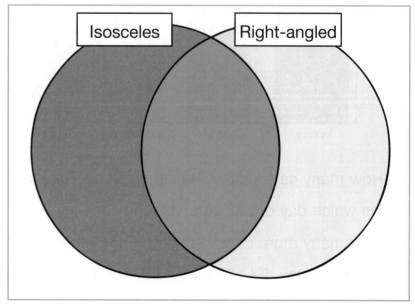

Isosceles   Right-angled

Equivalent fractions

Fractions that have the **same value** are called equivalent fractions.

$\frac{5}{10}$ is the same as $\frac{1}{2}$

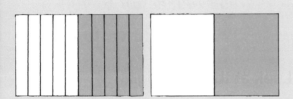

$\frac{1}{3}$ is the same as $\frac{2}{6}$

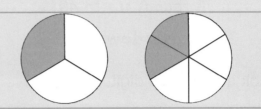

---

1 Complete the equivalent fractions. In a-d use the diagrams to help you complete the first fraction.

a 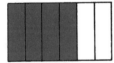 $\frac{\square}{6} = \frac{\square}{3}$

e $\frac{1}{\square} = \frac{2}{8}$ h $\frac{2}{\square} = \frac{4}{10}$

b  $\frac{\square}{10} = \frac{\square}{5}$

f $\frac{4}{12} = \frac{1}{\square}$ i $\frac{6}{\square} = \frac{1}{2}$

c $\frac{\square}{8} = \frac{\square}{2}$

g $\frac{\square}{10} = \frac{1}{2}$ j $\frac{\square}{4} = \frac{9}{12}$

d $\frac{\square}{8} = \frac{\square}{4}$

---

2 Cross out the fraction that is not equivalent to the others in each set.

a $\frac{1}{2}$ →

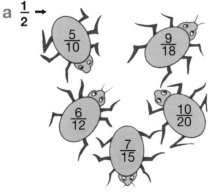

b $\frac{1}{4}$ →

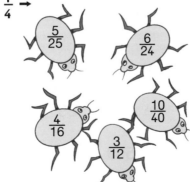

c $\frac{1}{3}$ →

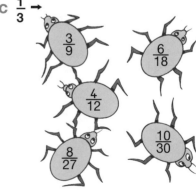

23

Rounding numbers

Rounding to the nearest 10	Rounding to the nearest 100
38 rounds **up** to 40	653 rounds **up** to 700
214 rounds **down** to 210	439 rounds **down** to 400

Look at the **ones** digit.

- If it is 5 or more, round up to the next tens digit.
- If it is less than 5, the tens digit stays the same.

Look at the **tens** digit.

- If it is 5 or more, round up to the next hundreds digit.
- If it is less than 5, the hundreds digit stays the same.

1 This chart shows a list of some of the highest waterfalls in the world. Round each height to the nearest 10 m and 100 m.

Rounded to the:

Waterfall	Country	Total drop (m)	Nearest 10 m	Nearest 100 m
Angel	Venezuela	979	_____	_____
Tugela	South Africa	947	_____	_____
Mongefossen	Norway	774	_____	_____
Yosemite	USA	739	_____	_____
Tyssestrengane	Norway	646	_____	_____
Sutherland	New Zealand	581	_____	_____
Kjellfossen	Norway	561	_____	_____

2 Round these to the nearest 10 or 100 to work out approximate answers.

a 73 + 89 → [   ]

b 17 × 9 → [   ]

c 346 − 152 → [   ]

d 509 + 296 → [   ]

e 256 + 799 → [   ]

f 509 − 296 → [   ]

Multiples

Multiples are the numbers in the **times tables**.

Multiples of 2 are 2, 4, 6, 8, 10, 12 and so on.

Multiples of 5 are 5, 10, 15, 20, 25 and so on.

Multiples of a number do not come to an end at ×12, they go on and on.
For example 52, 98, 114, 230 are all multiples of 2.

1 Write these numbers in the correct boxes. Some of them will belong in more than one box.

48 56 100 39 86 52 82 42 63 85 70 115 60 65

Multiples of 2	Multiples of 4	Multiples of 5	Multiples of 6

2 Colour all the multiples of 3 red.
Colour all the multiples of 5 blue.
What patterns do you see on the grid?

1	2	3	4	5	6	7	8	9	10
11	12	13	14	15	16	17	18	19	20
21	22	23	24	25	26	27	28	29	30
31	32	33	34	35	36	37	38	39	40
41	42	43	44	45	46	47	48	49	50
51	52	53	54	55	56	57	58	59	60
61	62	63	64	65	66	67	68	69	70
71	72	73	74	75	76	77	78	79	80
81	82	83	84	85	86	87	88	89	90
91	92	93	94	95	96	97	98	99	100

Money problems

If you need to find the **difference** between two amounts, count on from the lower amount.

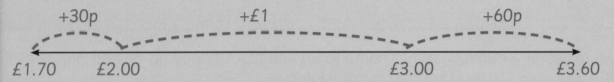

+30p   +£1   +60p

£1.70   £2.00   £3.00   £3.60

The difference between £1.70 and £3.60 is £1.90 (30p + £1 + 60p)

You can work out an amount of change in this way as well.

1 Work out these price differences.

a

£3.45   £1.70

Difference ▢

c

£1.96   £3.40

Difference ▢

e

£1.79   £2.07

Difference ▢

b

Ready Meal £1.40   £2.75 Fruit Cake

Difference ▢

d

£3.05   £1.60

Difference ▢

f

£2.84   £3.60

Difference ▢

2 Draw a line to join these price labels to the correct change from £10.

a £3.49 ○   **e** £7.59 ○

b £8.99 ○   **f** £8.89 ○

c £7.89 ○   **g** £7.39 ○

d £3.69 ○   **h** £6.59 ○

£1.01   £3.41
£2.11   £6.51   £1.11
£6.31   £2.41   £2.61

Angles

90° is a quarter turn, or a **right angle**.

An **acute angle** is less than 90°.

A **straight line** is 180°.

An **obtuse angle** is between 90° and 180°.

A circle is 360°.

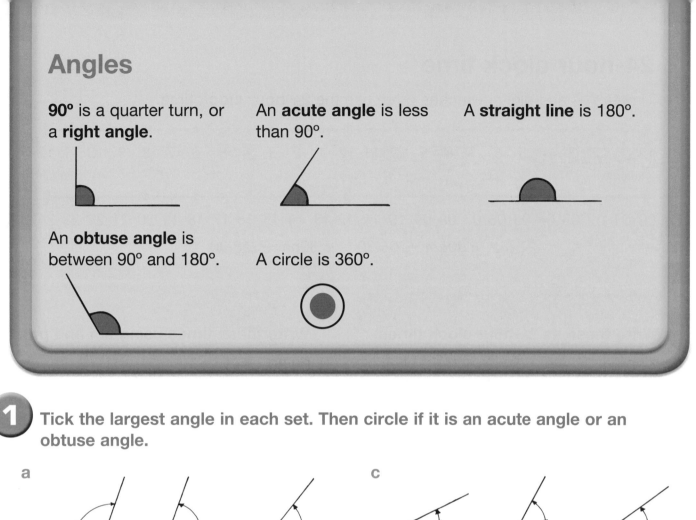

1 Tick the largest angle in each set. Then circle if it is an acute angle or an obtuse angle.

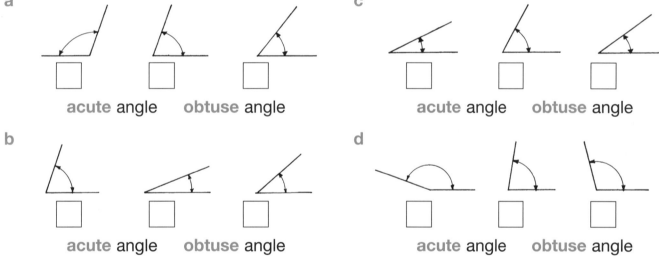

a
☐ ☐ ☐

    acute angle   obtuse angle

c
☐ ☐ ☐

    acute angle   obtuse angle

b
☐ ☐ ☐

    acute angle   obtuse angle

d
☐ ☐ ☐

    acute angle   obtuse angle

2 These are the eight compass directions. Write the direction you will face after turning.

a Start facing north. Turn 90° clockwise. _____

b Start facing west. Turn 180° anticlockwise. _____

c Start facing south. Turn 45° clockwise. _____

d Start facing east. Turn 360° anticlockwise. _____

e Start facing north-east. Turn 90° clockwise. _____

f Start facing north-west. Turn 45° anticlockwise. _____

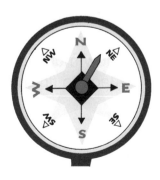

24-hour clock time

Timetables and digital watches often use the **24-hour clock** time.

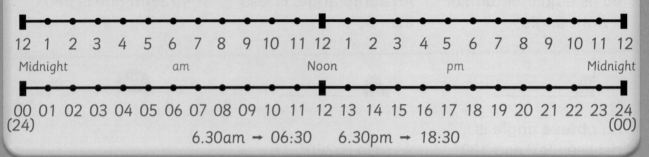

6.30am → 06:30   6.30pm → 18:30

1 Write these as 24-hour clock times.

a 7.30am → [ ]

b 9.00pm → [ ]

c 10.15am → [ ]

d 4.45pm → [ ]

e 2.10am → [ ]

f 11.50pm → [ ]

Write these times using am and pm.

g 09:30 → [ ]

h 15:00 → [ ]

i 20:15 → [ ]

j 13:40 → [ ]

k 10:55 → [ ]

l 22:20 → [ ]

2 Answer these questions about the marathon race.

a How long did it take Tom to run the race?

_____

b How long did it take Jill to run the race

_____

c How long did it take Jack to run the race?

_____

d How much longer did Jill take than Jack to finish the race?

_____

RESULTS		
Name	**Start Time**	**Finish Time**
Tom	10:20	14:35
Jill	10:25	14:05
Jack	10:30	13:20

Handling data

Data can be shown on graphs.
Graphs have **axes** and a **scale**.

Read the scale and labels on the axes carefully.

Vertical axis

Horizontal axis

Books sold from a bookshop in 1 week

Number of books

Mon Tues Wed Thurs Fri Sat

Day

1 Look at the graph above and answer these.

a How many books were sold on Thursday?   _____

b On which day were 22 books sold?   _____

c How many more books were sold on
   Friday than on Monday?   _____

d On which day did the bookshop sell half the
   number of books sold on Thursday?   _____

e On Saturday, the bookshop sold as many books
   as the total number of books sold on Monday and
   Tuesday. Show this on the graph.   _____

f How many books were sold in total in the week,
   including Saturday?   _____

2 Carry out a word survey. Choose a page from one of your books. Count the
number of letters for each word and record it on this tally chart. Show your
results on a bar chart.

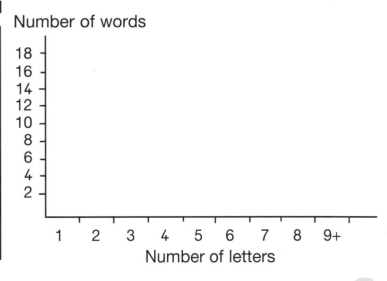

Number of letters for each word

1	
2	
3	
4	
5	
6	
7	
8	
9+	

Number of words

18
16
14
12
10
8
6
4
2

1   2   3   4   5   6   7   8   9+

Number of letters

Problems

When you read a **word problem**, try to 'picture' the problem.

Try these four steps.

1 Read the problem
What do you need to find out?

2 Sort out the calculation
There may be one or more parts to the question. What calculations are needed?

3 Work out the answer
Will you use a mental or written method?

4 Check back
Read the question again. Have you answered it fully?

1 Read these word problems and answer them.

a A bar of chocolate costs 45p. What do 4 bars cost? _____

b Sophie has 90 g of butter. She uses 35 g to make a loaf of bread. How much butter is left? _____

c A board game costs £8.40. It is reduced by £2.50 in a sale. What is the new price of the game? _____

d 68 people are going on a trip. Minibuses can t ake 10 people. How many minibuses will be needed? _____

e A pencil costs 19p. How many can be bought for £2? _____

f Daniel is saving up to buy a game for £42. He has £10. 50 and his uncle gives him £15. How much more does he need to save? _____

g Mrs Benson travels 48 km each day to get to work and back. How far will she travel in 5 days? _____

h Jack had 18 stickers. He bought 16 more, then he gave half of his stickers to his brother. How many did he give to his brother? _____

2 These are the ingredients of a chocolate cake for four people. Write the ingredients needed for a chocolate cake for 12 people.

50 g margarine
40 g sugar
60 g flour
1 egg
15 g cocoa powder
20 ml milk

_____
_____
_____
_____
_____
_____

Coordinates

Coordinates help to **find a position** on a grid.

Look at the coordinates of A and B.

Read the numbers across **horizontally** and then up **vertically** for the pair of coordinates. (2,6) and (7,3)

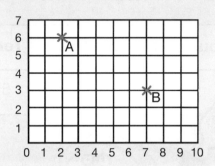

1 Look at the grid below and answer the questions.

a What letter is at position:

(2,3) ____   (8,2) ____   (10,9) ____

b What are the coordinates for

D (____,____)   A (____,____)   S (____,____)

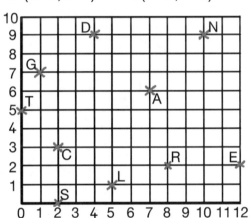

c Use the coordinates to spell out a shape and draw it in the box below.

(8,2) (12,2) (2,3) (0,5) (7,6)
(10,9) (1,7) (5,1) (12,2)

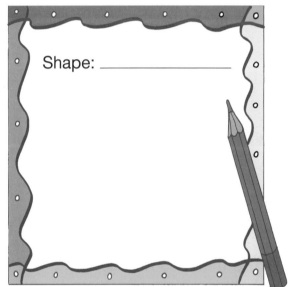

Shape: _____

2 Draw a quadrilateral on this grid.

The coordinates are:

(4,2) (6,5) (3,7) (1,4)

The shape is a _____.

Move two of the coordinates to make the shape into a rectangle.

Write the coordinates of your rectangle.

_____ _____

_____ _____

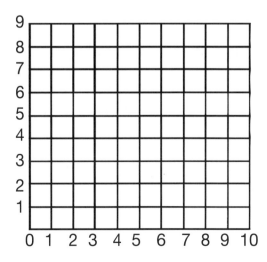

Test 1 Place value (1)

Thousands	Hundreds	Tens	Units	
4	9	5	7	= 4000 + 900 + 50 + 7

Write the missing numbers.

1. 4173 = 4000 + 100 + ☐ + 3

2. 8465 = ☐ + 400 + 60 + 5

3. 3657 = 3000 + ☐ + 50 + 7

4. 7895 = 7000 + 800 + ☐ + 5

5. 6218 = ☐ + 200 + 10 + 8

Write these as numbers.

6. two thousand one hundred and eight ☐

7. four thousand and ninety ☐

8. seven thousand two hundred and thirty-five ☐

9. three thousand eight hundred and sixteen ☐

10. nine thousand seven hundred ☐

Colour in your score

32

Test 2 Addition and subtraction (1)

Adding words

altogether TOTAL sum
add more than
increase plus

Subtracting words

less than take away
minus subtract FEWER
decrease difference

Work out the answers.

1. Add 353 to 34.

2. Total 35, 62 and 101.

3. What is the difference between 476 and 500?

4. Decrease 382 by 182.

5. What is 604 take away 418?

6. What change would you get from £5 after spending £3.44?

7. Total 1·6 m, 2·5 m and 4·1 m.

8. There were 225 ml of liquid in a jug and 60 ml was poured out. How much liquid was left?

9. Add £1.23, £2.75 and £1.35.

10. You have a 5·2 m strip of ribbon. You need 1·75 m to wrap your parcel. How much ribbon would be left?

10 9 8 7 6 5 4 3 2 1

Colour in your score

Test 3 **Measures**

1 centimetre = 10 millimetres	1 litre = 1000 millilitres
1 cm = 10 mm	1 l = 1000 ml
1 metre = 100 centimetres	1 kilogram = 1000 grams
1 m = 100 cm	1 kg = 1000 g
1 kilometre = 1000 metres	
1 km = 1000 m	

Answer these questions.

1. $\frac{1}{2}$ m = ◻ cm

4. $\frac{1}{4}$ l = ◻ ml

2. $\frac{1}{2}$ cm = ◻ mm

5. $\frac{1}{4}$ kg = ◻ g

3. $\frac{1}{10}$ km = ◻ m

Measure these lines with a ruler.

6. ◻ mm

7. ◻ mm

8. ◻ mm

9. ◻ mm

10. ◻ mm

Colour in your score

34

Test 4 2-D shapes

A **polygon** is any 2-D shape with straight sides.

A **regular polygon's** sides and angles are all equal.

How many sides have each of these shapes?

1. A quadrilateral has [ ] sides.

2. An octagon has [ ] sides.

3. A hexagon has [ ] sides.

4. A triangle has [ ] sides.

5. A pentagon has [ ] sides.

Name these shapes.

6. _____

7. _____

8. 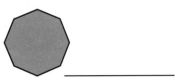 _____

9. _____

10. _____

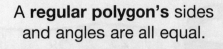

Colour in your score

Test 5 Number sequences

Number patterns can go up or down.

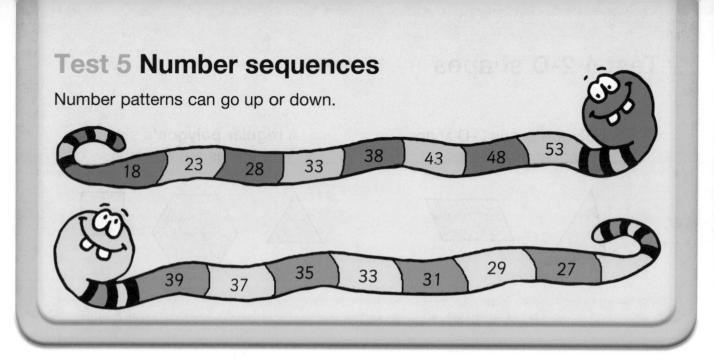

Write the missing numbers in these sequences.

1.

| 32 | 35 | 38 | | 44 | 47 | 50 | 53 | | 59 |

2.

| 48 | 52 | | 60 | 64 | 68 | | 76 | 80 | 84 |

3.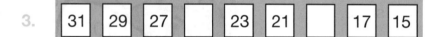

| 31 | 29 | 27 | | 23 | 21 | | 17 | 15 |

4.

| 230 | 210 | | 170 | 150 | | 110 | 90 | 70 |

5.

| 76 | 81 | 86 | 91 | | 101 | 106 | | 116 |

Write the missing numbers on these number lines.

6.   7.

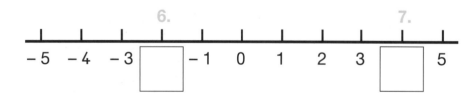

– 5   – 4   – 3   ☐   – 1   0   1   2   3   ☐   5

8.   9.   10.

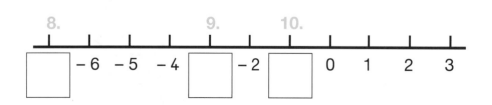

☐   – 6   – 5   – 4   ☐   – 2   ☐   0   1   2   3

10
9
8
7
6
5
4
3
2
1

Colour in your score

36

Test 6 Multiplication tables

You need to know your **tables**.

Remember, **4 × 6** is the same as **6 × 4**.

It doesn't matter which way round you multiply.

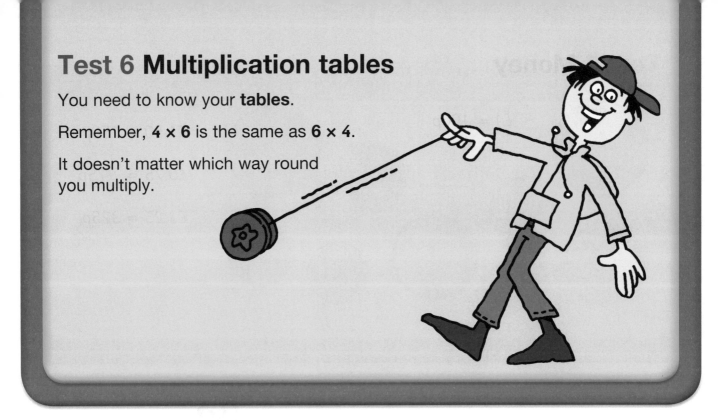

Write the missing numbers.

1. $7 \times \boxed{} = 35$

2. $\boxed{} \times 4 = 44$

3. $8 \times 3 = \boxed{}$

4. $\boxed{} \times 7 = 28$

5. $12 \times \boxed{} = 60$

6. $8 \times \boxed{} = 40$

7. $11 \times 6 = \boxed{}$

8. $\boxed{} \times 3 = 27$

9. $\boxed{} \times 6 = 72$

10. $4 \times \boxed{} = 36$

Colour in your score

Test 7 Money

£1 = 100p

£1.50 = 150p

£0.75 = 75p

£3.25 = 325p

Convert these amounts into pounds or pence.

1. £2.35 = ☐ p

2. £6.45 = ☐ p

3. £ ☐ = 370p

4. £1.09 = ☐ p

5. £ ☐ = 214p

6. £2.75 = ☐ p

Write the totals.

7. £1.85 ▪ + 70p ▪ = £ ☐

8. 65p ▪ + £2.50 ▪ = £ ☐

9. 90p ▪ + £3.15 ▪ = £ ☐

10. £1.90 ▪ + £2.20 ▪ = £ ☐

Colour in your score

38

Test 8 **Fractions**

Fractions which are the same value are called **equivalent fractions**.

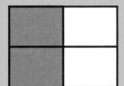 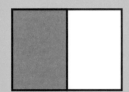  

$\frac{2}{4}$ is the same as $\frac{1}{2}$ $\qquad$ $\frac{1}{3}$ is the same as $\frac{2}{6}$

Write the fractions which are shaded.

1. 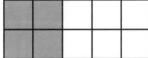 $\frac{\square}{10} = \frac{\square}{5}$

2. $\frac{\square}{6} = \frac{\square}{2}$

3. 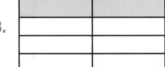 $\frac{\square}{8} = \frac{\square}{4}$

4. 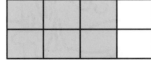 $\frac{\square}{8} = \frac{\square}{4}$

5. $\frac{\square}{8} = \frac{\square}{2}$

Complete these fractions.

6. $\frac{4}{5} = \frac{8}{\square}$ $\qquad$ 8. $\frac{1}{\square} = \frac{3}{12}$ $\qquad$ 10. $\frac{3}{10} = \frac{6}{\square}$

7. $\frac{2}{3} = \frac{\square}{9}$ $\qquad$ 9. $\frac{3}{4} = \frac{\square}{12}$

Colour in your score

Test 9 Time

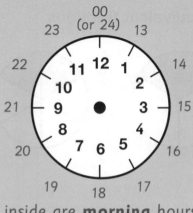

inside are **morning** hours
outside are **afternoon** hours

am times	pm times
morning hours	afternoon hours
midnight ⟶ noon ⟶ midnight	

Join the matching times.

1. | 10:25 | 11.10 pm

2. | 18:30 | 6.15 am

3. | 23:10 | 10.25 am

4. | 06:15 | 12.45 am

5. | 00:45 | 6.30 pm

Write each time in the 24-hour clock time.

6.   4.30 pm ⟹ ____ .

7.   6.25 am ⟹ ____ .

8.   5.15 pm ⟹ ____ .

9.   10.20 am ⟹ ____ .

10.   11.55 pm ⟹ ____ .

Colour in your score

40

Test 10 Data handling (1)

This **pictogram** shows information about 4 buses that make the same journey at different times.

Bus	Number of people on each bus
A	☆ ☆ ⧆
B	☆ ☆
C	☆ ☆ ☆ ☆ ☆ ⧆
D	☆ ☆ ☆

☆ 5 people

⧆ 1 to 4 people

Passengers on bus C

Adults Children Babies

😀 = 2 people   🙂 = 1 person

Use the information above to answer these questions.

1. How many people travelled on bus B? ☐

2. How many people travelled on bus D? ☐

3. Approximately how many people travelled on bus A? ☐ to ☐ people

4. How many people travelled on bus C? ☐ people

5. Approximately how many people travelled altogether on all 4 buses? ☐ to ☐ people

6. How many adults travelled on bus C? ☐

7. How many children travelled on bus C? ☐

8. How many babies travelled on bus C? ☐

9. How many more adults than children travelled on bus C? ☐

10. How many people travelled altogether on bus C? ☐

Colour in your score

41

Test 11 Multiplying and dividing by 10

To **multiply by 10**, move all the digits to the **left**. The empty place is filled by a zero.

$$75 \times 10 = $$
$$750$$

To **divide by 10**, move all the digits one place to the **right**.

$$230 \div 10 = $$
$$23$$

Multiply each of these numbers by 10.

1. 45   x 10 ⟹
2. 63   x 10 ⟹
3. 81   x 10 ⟹
4. 107   x 10 ⟹
5. 234   x 10 ⟹

Divide each of these numbers by 10.

6. 53   ÷10 ⟹
7. 470   ÷10 ⟹
8. 380   ÷10 ⟹
9. 635   ÷10 ⟹
10. 8010   ÷10 ⟹

Colour in your score

42

Test 12 Addition

Use mental methods to answer these.

1.   148 + 30 =

2.   36 + 323 =

3.   444 + 146 =

4.   138 + 700 =

5.   5610 + 29 =

6.   48 + 3037 =

7.   8100 + 763 =

8.   7210 + 490 =

9.   8139 + 1045 =

10.   1057 + 1074 =

Colour in your score

43

Test 13 Money: adding coins

When adding coins, start with the **highest value** coins to make it easier.

Write these totals using decimal notation.

1. £1 20p 20p 50p 2p ⇨ ☐

2. £1 £1 20p 50p 10p ⇨ ☐

3. 50p 20p £2 2p 5p ⇨ ☐

4. 10p 1p 2p £2 £2 ⇨ ☐

5. 10p 50p 2p 5p £1 ⇨ ☐

Which coins would you use to buy these books to give the exact money? Use the smallest possible number of coins.

6. £4.90 _____

7. £3.50 _____

8. £1.13 _____

9. £2.26 _____

10. £4.14 _____

Colour in your score

Test 14 Measures problems

When solving **measures problems**, make sure you read the questions carefully and then work out what calculations you need to do.

C 192 cm

D 240 cm

A 135 cm

B 155 cm

Use the information above to answer these questions.

1. What is the difference in length between the longest and shortest ropes?
   [ ] cm

2. How much longer is rope C than rope B?
   [ ] cm

3. What is the total length of ropes A and B?
   [ ] cm

4. Which rope is 85 cm longer than rope B?
   [ ]

5. Which rope can be cut into 5 equal lengths of 27 cm?
   [ ]

Work out the answers to these problems.

6. A chef has a 630 g bag of flour and uses 85 g. How much flour is left in the bag?
   [ ] g

7. Alex drove 5800 km in one year and 7600 km the following year. How much further did he drive in the second year?
   [ ] km

8. If 38 g of cake mixture is needed to make 1 cake, how much is needed to make 6 cakes?
   [ ] g

9. Vikram swam 850 m for a sponsored swim. He swam in widths of 10 m. How many widths did he swim?
   [ ]

10. A pack of 6 cartons has 1260 ml of drinks in total. A can holds 240 ml. Which holds more, a can or a carton?
    [ ]

10
9
8
7
6
5
4
3
2
1

Colour in your score

45

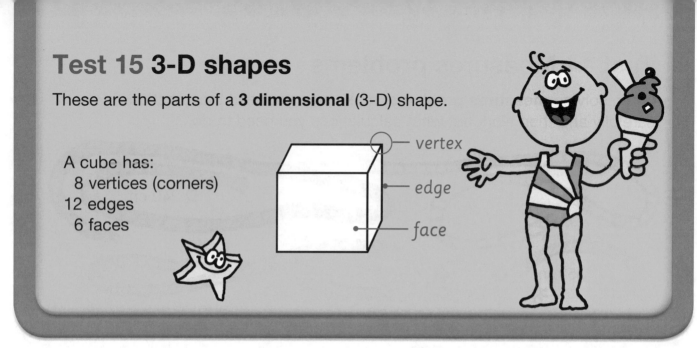

Test 15 3-D shapes

These are the parts of a **3 dimensional** (3-D) shape.

A cube has:
- 8 vertices (corners)
- 12 edges
- 6 faces

vertex

edge

face

Name each shape. Write the missing numbers of corners, edges or faces.

1. name _____

2.
vertices

8
edges

3.
faces

4. name _____

0
vertices

5.
edges

6.
faces

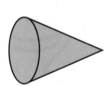

7. name _____

1
vertices

1
edges

8.
faces

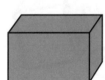

9. name _____

8
vertices

12
edges

10.
faces

Colour in your score

46

Test 16 Number patterns

Look for number patterns.

1	2	3	4	5	6
7	8	9	10	11	12
13	14	15	16	17	18
19	20	21	22	23	24
25	26	27	28	29	30
31	32	33	34	35	36

Write the next number in each number pattern.

1. | 12 | 14 | 16 | 18 | 20 | |

2. | 15 | 18 | 21 | 24 | 27 | |

3. | 9 | 11 | 13 | 15 | 17 | |

4. | 33 | 30 | 27 | 24 | 21 | |

5. | 16 | 20 | 24 | 28 | 32 | |

Write the missing number in each number pattern.

6. | 22 | 20 | 18 | | 14 | 12 | 10 |

7. | 27 | 24 | | 18 | 15 | 12 | 9 |

8. | | 28 | 30 | 32 | 34 | 36 | 38 |

9. | 36 | 32 | 28 | | 20 | 16 | 12 |

10. | 9 | 12 | 15 | 18 | | 24 | 27 |

Colour in your score

Test 17 **Division**

The box opposite shows one way to divide 218 by 9.

		2	4	r	2	
9)	2	1	8			
−	1	8	0			→ (9 × 20)
		3	8			
	−	3	6			→ (9 × 4)
			2			remainder

Work out these division problems.

1. 478 ÷ 5 = ☐

2. 860 ÷ 7 = ☐

3. 577 ÷ 4 = ☐

4. 639 ÷ 9 = ☐

5. 877 ÷ 6 = ☐

Write the missing digit.

6.
```
    1  6  ☐
4) 6  7  6
```

7.
```
    7  7
5) 3  ☐  5
```

8.
```
    ☐  6
6) 3  9  6
```

9.
```
    2  7  5
3) ☐  2  5
```

10.
```
         3  1
☐) 2  1  7
```

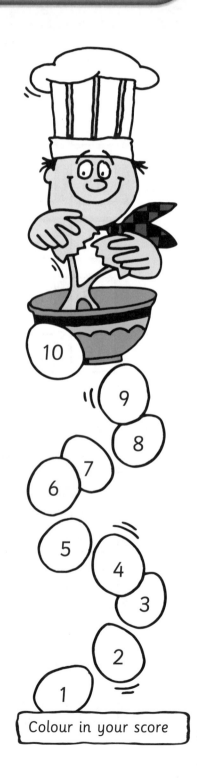

10
9
8
7
6
5
4
3
2
1

Colour in your score

48

Test 18 Money problems (1)

When finding the **difference** between two amounts, **count on** from the **lower** amount.

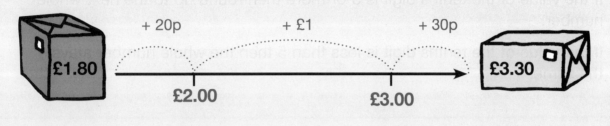

The **difference** between £1.80 and £3.30 is **£1.50** (20p + £1 + 30p).

Write the difference between these prices.

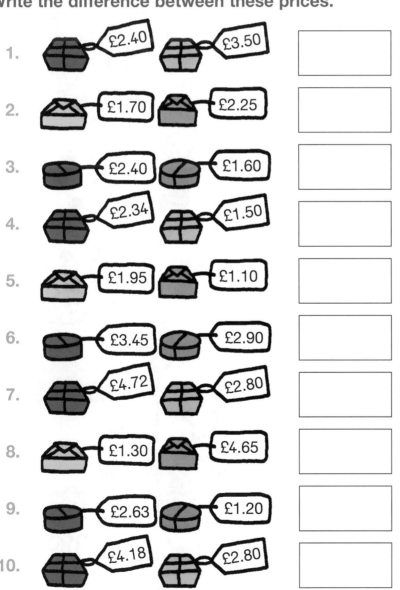

1. £2.40 £3.50

2. £1.70 £2.25

3. £2.40 £1.60

4. £2.34 £1.50

5. £1.95 £1.10

6. £3.45 £2.90

7. £4.72 £2.80

8. £1.30 £4.65

9. £2.63 £1.20

10. £4.18 £2.80

10
9
8
7
6
5
4
3
2
1

Colour in your score

49

Test 19 Rounding decimals

When rounding a decimal number to the nearest whole number look at the value of the tenths.

6.3 rounds **down** to 6

6.7 rounds **up** to 7

If the value of the tenths digit is 5 or more then round up to the next whole number.

If the value of the tenths digit is less than 5 then the whole number stays the same.

Write these numbers using decimals.

1. four point one six

2. fourteen point zero five

3. nought point two four

4. six and three hundredths

5. nine and nine tenths

Round these decimal numbers to the nearest whole number.

6. 5·6

7. 1·5

8. 0·6

9. 3·7

10. 4·2

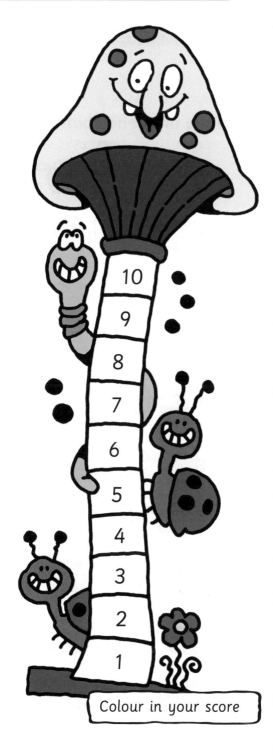

10
9
8
7
6
5
4
3
2
1

Colour in your score

50

Test 20 Data handling (2)

The numbers 1-10 have been sorted on these two diagrams.

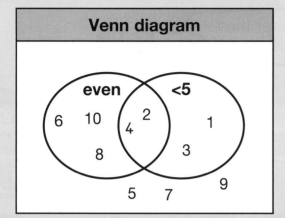

	Venn diagram		Carroll diagram	

Venn diagram

even   <5

6   10   2   1
    4
  8   3
    5   7   9

Carroll diagram

	even	not even
<5	2 4	1 3
not <5	6 10 8	5 9 7

Write the numbers in the correct place on each diagram.

> means greater than
< means less than

1.   7

2.   31

3.   28

4.   16

5.   19

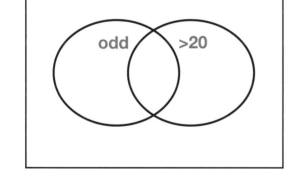

odd   >20

6.   24

7.   13

8.   15

9.   1

10.   6

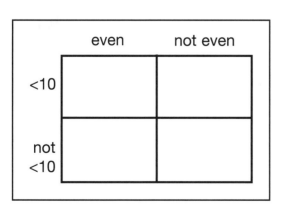

	even	not even
<10		
not <10		

Colour in your score

Test 21 Place value (2)

To help work out the **order of numbers**, you can write them in a list, lining up the units columns.

247 29 2403 249

2403
249
247
29

> greater than
< less than

Write the signs > or < for each pair of numbers.

1. 6093 ☐ 6103

2. 4206 ☐ 4311

3. 7415 ☐ 7409

4. 2046 ☐ 2050

5. 8114 ☐ 8108

Write the numbers in order starting with the smallest.

6. 318 308 381 310 ☐ ☐ ☐ ☐

7. 4081 4180 4191 4008 ☐ ☐ ☐ ☐

8. 6095 6293 6120 6905 ☐ ☐ ☐ ☐

9. 2140 2004 410 4010 ☐ ☐ ☐ ☐

10. 9214 902 9189 989 ☐ ☐ ☐ ☐

Colour in your score

Test 22 Addition and subtraction (2)

Some questions are easier to work out in your head than writing them down.

It is quicker to answer 386 − 99 mentally than as a written calculation.

See which of these you can answer in your head.

1. Total 437 and 59.

2. Take 66 away from 385.

3. 3765 add 200.

4. 5793 subtract 50.

5. Increase 472 by 84.

Write the missing numbers.

6. 3·7 + ☐ = 5

7. 3 − ☐ = 1·5

8. 125 + ☐ = 500

9. 1000 − ☐ = 225

10. ☐ + 550 = 1000

Colour in your score

53

Test 23 Perimeter

	1	2	3	4	5
18					6
17					7
16					8
15					9
	14	13	12	11	10

Count the number of squares along each side.
Perimeter = 18 cm

Perimeter is the distance around a two dimensional shape.

7 m

5 m

To find the perimeter add up the length of each side

7 m + 7 m + 5 m + 5 m = 24 m

Find the perimeter of each of these shapes, in squares.

1. 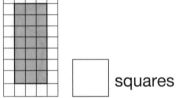 ☐ squares

4. 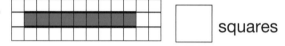 ☐ squares

2. 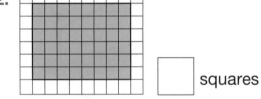 ☐ squares

5. 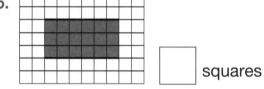 ☐ squares

3. 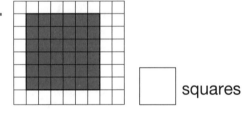 ☐ squares

6.  ☐ squares

Now try these with answers in centimetres or metres.

7.
9 cm
5 cm
☐ cm

9.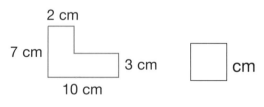
2 cm
7 cm
3 cm
10 cm
☐ cm

8.
5 m
6 m
☐ m

10.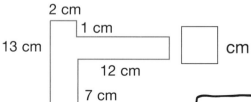
2 cm
1 cm
13 cm
12 cm
7 cm
☐ cm

Colour in your score

10
9
8
7
6
5
4
3
2
1

Test 24 Shape: symmetry

A shape has line **symmetry** if both sides are exactly the same when a mirror line is drawn.

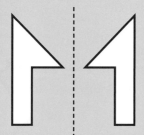  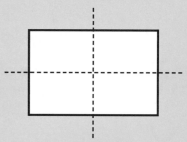

A shape reflected in a mirror.   1 line of symmetry.   2 lines of symmetry.

Draw the reflection of each shape.

1. 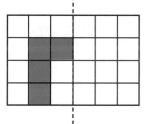   2. 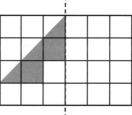   3.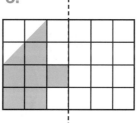

4. 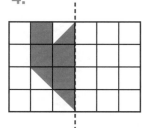   5.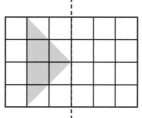

Draw the lines of symmetry on each shape.

6. 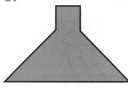   7. 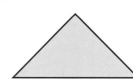   8.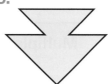

9.   10.

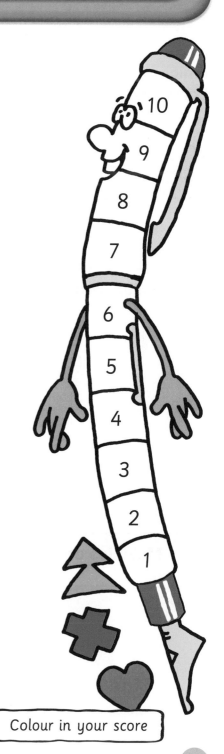

Colour in your score

Test 25 **Multiples**

Multiples of 2 are: 2, 4, 6, 8, 10, 12... and so on.

Multiples of 3 are: 3, 6, 9, 12, 15, 18... and so on.

Multiples of a number do not come to an end at ×12, they go on and on. So, for example, 82, 94, 106 and 300 are all multiples of 2.

Which of these numbers are multiples of 2, 3, 4 or 5?
Some numbers are used more than once.

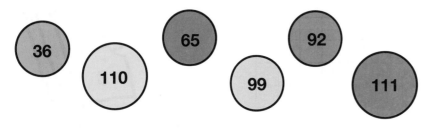

Multiples of 2	Multiples of 3
1.	4.
2.	5.
3.	6.

Multiples of 4	Multiples of 5
7.	9.
8.	10.

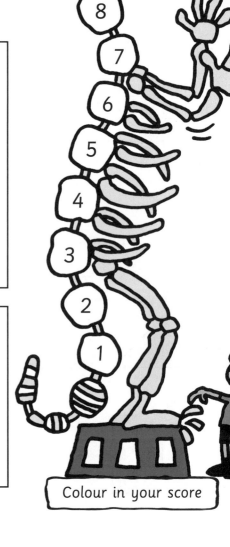

Colour in your score

56

Test 26 Multiplication and division

The opposite, or inverse, of
multiplication is division.

24 x 3 = 72   so   72 ÷ 3 = 24

The opposite, or inverse, of
division is multiplication.

75 ÷ 5 = 15   so   15 x 5 = 75

Complete the number machine tables.

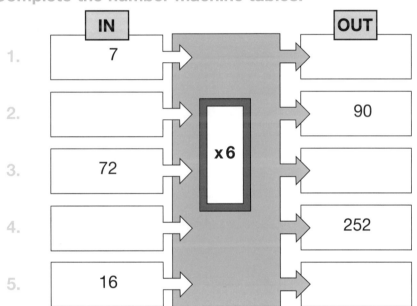

	IN		OUT
1.	7	x6	
2.			90
3.	72		
4.			252
5.	16		

Write the missing numbers.

6.   40   ×   [   ]   =   240

7.   800   ÷   [   ]   =   40

8.   30   ×   [   ]   =   1500

9.   60   ÷   [   ]   =   2

10.   50   ×   [   ]   =   450

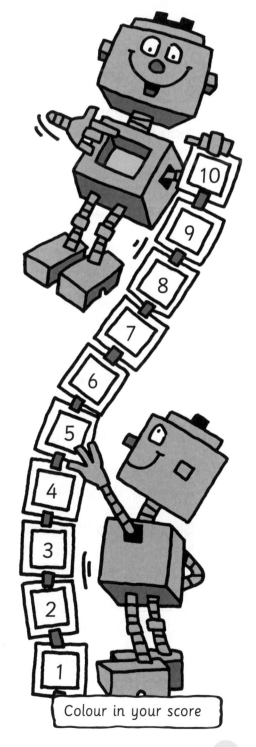

Colour in your score

Test 27 Money problems (2)

When working out **word problems**, read the questions carefully to work out the calculations you need to do.

Answer these problems.

1. Amy has 95p and spends 57p. How much money does she have left?

2. A cinema ticket costs £3.50 for an adult and £3 for a child. What is the total cost for 2 adults and 2 children?

3. A newspaper costs 35p. What is the cost for a week's supply of newspapers?

4. A sweet costs 14p. How many can be bought for £1?

5. A bus journey costs £1.20. How much will the total fare be for 4 people?

6. A car costs £2400. If it is reduced by £800, how much will it cost?

7. A book costs £4.70. It is reduced by £1.90 in a sale. What is the new price of the book?

8. Sam has two 20p coins and a 50p coin. He buys a magazine at 72p. How much money does he have left?

9. What is the total cost of a £4.50 T-shirt and a £3.70 pair of shorts?

10. If a fairground ride costs 80p, what is the cost of 3 rides?

Colour in your score

58

Test 28 Decimals

hundreds		tens		ones		(decimal point)		tenths		hundredths
2		4		3		•		2		5
200	+	40	+	3	+			$\frac{2}{10}$	+	$\frac{5}{100}$

Write in words the value of the bold digits in these numbers.

1. 3**5**·3

2. 274·2**1**

3. 0·**37**

4. **27**·3

5. 462·**9**

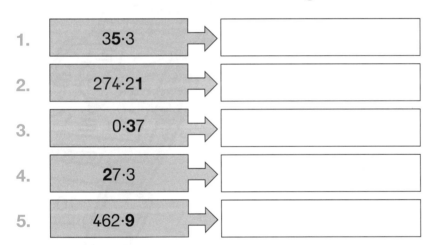

Write the number each arrow points to.

6.

7.

8.

9.

10.

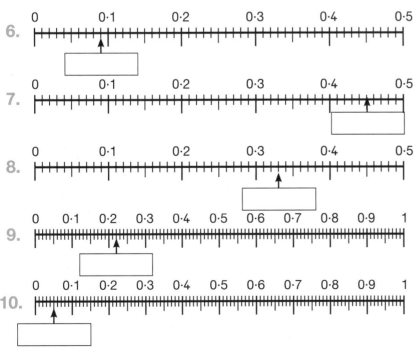

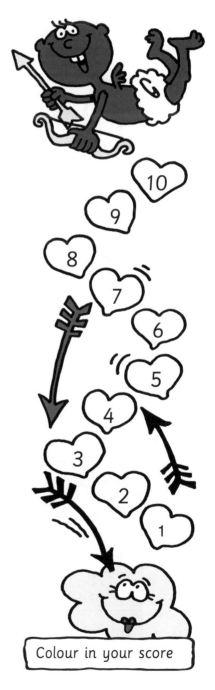

Colour in your score

59

Test 29 Time problems

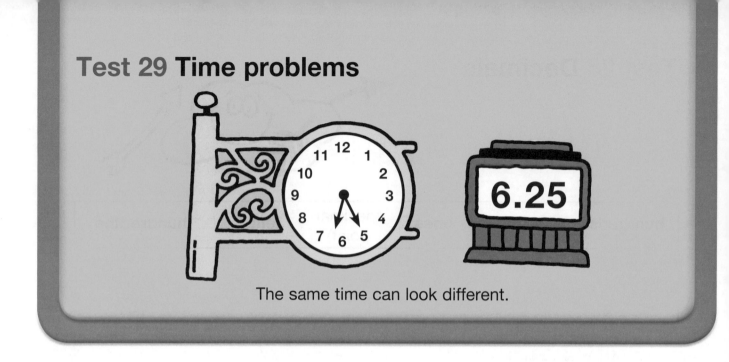

6.25

The same time can look different.

These clocks are 45 minutes fast.
Write the real time for each of them.

1.

4.

2.

5.

3.

A train takes 20 minutes between each of these stations.
Complete the timetable.

6.	Smedley	2.10	
7.	Chadwick		4.45
8.	Welby	2.50	
9.	Burnsford		5.25
10.	Ragby		5.45

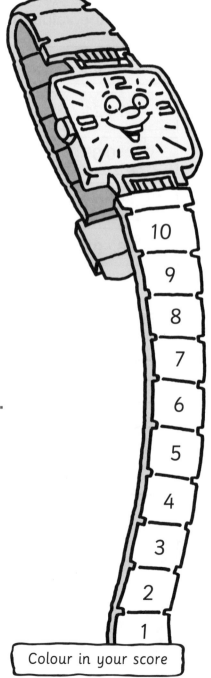

10
9
8
7
6
5
4
3
2
1

Colour in your score

Test 30 Data handling (3)

These **graphs** show the number of cans collected by two classes in a school over a month.

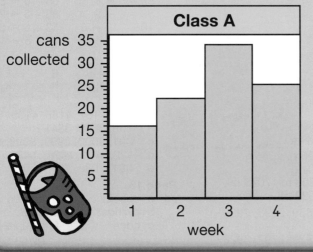

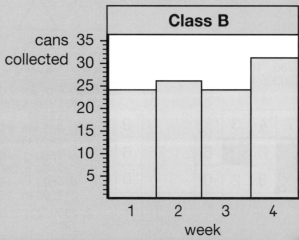

Answer these problems.

1. How many cans were collected by Class A in week 2?

2. How many cans were collected by Class B in week 1?

3. In which week did Class A collect 25 cans?

4. How many more cans were collected in week 1 by Class B than by Class A?

5. In which week did Class A collect 10 more cans than Class B?

6. In which week did Class B collect 26 cans?

7. In which 2 weeks were the same number of cans collected by Class B?

8. How many fewer cans were collected in week 4 by Class A than Class B?

9. How many cans altogether were collected by Class B?

10. Which class collected the most cans?

Colour in your score

ANSWERS

Page 2
1. **a** 758, 759, 760
   b 618, 608, 598
   c 506, 516, 526
   d 1641, 2641, 3641
   e 285, 185, 85
   f 8030, 7030, 6030

2.

¹7	²4	3			⁷9
³3	■	0	■	⁴6	6
5	■	⁵9	2	0	0
1			⁶8	0	7	4

Page 3
The missing numbers are:
1. **a** 50, 125, 150, 175   rule +25
   b 24, 30, 36, 48   rule +6
   c 9, 27, 54, 63   rule +9
   d 21, 42, 49, 56   rule +7
   e 3000, 4000, 5000,   rule +1000
      7000
   f 54, 60, 72, 90   rule +6
2. **a** −4, −3, −1, 1, 2
   b −3, −2, −1, 2, 3
   c −7, −6, −5, −3, −1, 0
   d −2, −1, 0, 1, 2, 4

Page 4
1. **a** 5 tens   **g** 9 ones
   b 6 thousands   **h** 7 hundreds
   c 8 ones   **i** 3 tens
   d 2 hundreds   **j** 4 ones
   e 6 tens   **k** 8 thousands
   f 5 thousands   **l** 7 hundreds
2. **a** 400   **f** 5000
   b 800   **g** 3000
   c 400   **h** 3000
   d 400   **i** 5000
   e 500   **j** 9000

Page 5
1. **a** 54 and 86   **d** 229
   b 540   **e** 124 and 86
   c 154   **f** 419
2. **a** 8262   **e** £46.44
   b 11923   **f** £136.05
   c 6063   **g** £48.75
   d 9025   **h** £66.40

Page 6
1. **a** triangle ✔   **g** quadrilateral
   b octagon ✔   **h** pentagon ✔
   c pentagon   **i** hexagon ✔
   d octagon   **j** decagon
   e heptagon   **k** nonagon
   f hexagon   **l** triangle
2. For a, b, c, d and h, there are
   many possible answers. Check
   each shape has the correct
   number of sides.
   d Check there is a right angle.
   e

f

g

Page 7
1. **a** £958, £1090, £1900, £2589,
      £2850
   b 965 km, 2830 km, 3095 km,
      3520 km, 3755 km
   c 1599 g, 1995 g, 2046 g,
      2460 g, 2604 g
   d 4599 ml, 4600 ml, 7025 ml,
      7028 ml, 7529 ml
2. 2389, 2398, 2839, 2893, 2938,
   2983
   3289, 3298, 3829, 3892, 3928,
   3982
   8239, 8293, 8329, 8392, 8923,
   8932
   9238, 9283, 9328, 9382, 9823,
   9832

Page 8
1. **a**

b
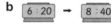

c

d

2. **a** 15 minutes   **d** 15 minutes
   b 25 minutes   **e** 20 minutes
   c 5 minutes   **f** 25 minutes

Page 9
1. **a** $\frac{8}{10} = \frac{4}{5}$ **f** 9
   b $\frac{4}{12} = \frac{1}{3}$ **g** 5
   c $\frac{6}{8} = \frac{3}{4}$ **h** 5
   d $\frac{9}{15} = \frac{3}{5}$ **i** 18
   e 2   **j** 4
2. **a** $\frac{1}{10}$, $\frac{2}{10}$, $\frac{1}{4}$, $\frac{1}{2}$, $\frac{3}{5}$, $\frac{2}{3}$, $\frac{3}{4}$, $\frac{9}{10}$

Page 10
1. **a** 3500 m   **f** 6.5 or $6\frac{1}{2}$ km
   b 4 cm   **g** 220 mm
   c 1.5 or $1\frac{1}{2}$ m   **h** 18 000 m
   d 80 mm   **i** 475 cm
   e 25 cm   **j** 6.5 or $6\frac{1}{2}$ cm
2. **a** 45 mm   **d** 37 mm
   b 62 mm   **e** 71 mm
   c 58 mm

Page 11
1. **a** 3 × 8 = 24   **c** 6
      8 × 3 = 24   **d** 21
      24 ÷ 3 = 8   **e** 6
      24 ÷ 8 = 3   **f** 12
   b 7 × 4 = 28   **g** 4
      4 × 7 = 28   **h** 5
      28 ÷ 4 = 7   **i** 77
      28 ÷ 7 = 4   **j** 8
2. 60 ÷ 9 → 6   37 ÷ 3 → 1
   93 ÷ 10 → 3   48 ÷ 5 → 3

89 ÷ 5 → 4   65 ÷ 6 → 5
38 ÷ 6 → 2   80 ÷ 3 → 2
106 ÷ 10 → 6   53 ÷ 6 → 5
61 ÷ 2 → 1   46 ÷ 6 → 4

Page 12
1. **a** >   **d** <   **g** >   **j** >
   b <   **e** >   **h** <   **k** <
   c >   **f** >   **i** <   **l** >
2. **a** 4168, 4167, 4166, 4165
   b 3839, 3840, 3841
   c 9001, 9000, 8999, 8998, 8997
   d 4422, 4423, 4424, 4425
   e 7081, 7080, 7079, 7078, 7077

Page 13
1. **a** cuboid   **d** sphere
   b cylinder   **e** cube
   c cone   **f** (square-based)
      pyramid

2.

	faces	edges	vertices
a	5	8	5
b	6	12	8
c	5	9	6
d	4	6	4

Page 14
1. **a** 2 kg   **g** 10 000 g
   b 1500 g   **h** 6.75 or $6\frac{3}{4}$ kg
   c 5.5 or $5\frac{1}{2}$ kg   **i** 2500 g
   d 1.25 or $1\frac{1}{4}$ kg   **j** 4750 g
   e 7000 g   **k** 9.5 or $9\frac{1}{2}$ kg
   f 3250 g   **l** 1750 g
2. **a** 1.5 or $1\frac{1}{2}$ kg   **d** 650 g
   b 2.5 or $2\frac{1}{2}$ kg   **e** 1700 g
   c 0.5 or $\frac{1}{2}$ kg   **f** 600 g

Page 15
1. **a** 183   **d** 688   **g** 252
   b 77   **e** 968   **h** 1387
   c 369   **f** 173
2. These are possible answers
   a 9876 − 2345 = 7531
   b 6234 − 5987 = 247
   c 4935 − 2876 = 2059 or 4876 −
      2935 = 1941

Page 16
1. **a** 36 squares
   b 30 squares
   c 20 squares
2. Rectangles with the dimensions
   2 × 4 and 1 × 8.

Page 17
1. **a** 228   **e** 1314
   b 378   **f** 2268
   c 765   **g** 2048
   d 512   **h** 1420
2. **a** 189   **f** 691
   b 130 r 4   **g** 696
   c 181 r 2   **h** 438
   d 80 r 5   **i** 358
   e 602

Page 18
1. **a**

d

b 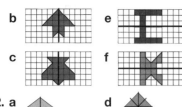 **e**

c **f**

2. a **d**

2 lines   4 lines
of symmetry   of symmetry

b   **e**

3 lines   5 lines
of symmetry   of symmetry

c

6 lines of symmetry

Page 19
1. a 3 l
   b 1500 ml
   c 6000 ml
   d 2.25 or $2\frac{1}{4}$ l
   e 1.75 or $1\frac{3}{4}$ l
   f 10 000 ml
   g 3500 ml
   h 2 l
   i 4.5 or $4\frac{1}{2}$ l
   j 8750 ml
   k 5.75 or $5\frac{3}{4}$ l
   l 6750 ml

2. a 500 ml
   b 750 ml
   c 100 ml
   d 250 ml
   e 1000 ml
   f 300 ml
   g 500 ml
   h 1500 ml

Page 20
1. a 0.3
   b 0.5
   c 0.2
   d 0.75
   e 0.17
   f 0.4
   g 0.41
   h 0.9
   i 0.65
   j 0.5
   k 0.59
   l 0.25

2. a 0.2, 0.4, 0.6, 0.7, 0.9
   b 3.1, 3.4, 3.6, 3.7, 3.9
   c 6.12, 6.14, 6.15, 6.17, 6.18

Page 21
1. a silver
   b 12
   c 10
   d blue
   e 9
   f 106

2. a 45
   b Thursday
   c 6
   d Wednesday

Page 22
1. a red
   b blue
   c yellow
   d red
   e blue
   f red
   g blue
   h yellow
   i yellow

2.
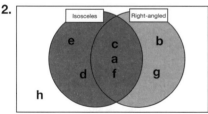

Page 23
1. a $\frac{4}{6} = \frac{2}{3}$
   b $\frac{6}{10} = \frac{3}{5}$
   c $\frac{4}{8} = \frac{1}{2}$
   d $\frac{6}{8} = \frac{3}{4}$
   e 4
   f 3
   g 5
   h 5
   i 12
   j 3

2. a $\frac{7}{15}$ **b** $\frac{5}{25}$ **c** $\frac{8}{27}$

Page 24
1.

Total drop (m)	Nearest 10 m	Nearest 100 m
979	980	1000
947	950	900
774	770	800
739	740	700
646	650	600
581	580	600
561	560	600

2. a 160
   b 200
   c 100
   d 800
   e 1100
   f 200

Page 25
1. Multiples of 2 – 48, 56, 100, 86, 52, 82, 42, 70, 60
Multiples of 6 – 48, 42, 60
Multiples of 4 – 48, 56, 100, 52, 60
Multiples of 5 – 100, 85, 70, 115, 60, 65

2. You can see these patterns:
The red squares make diagonal lines and the blue squares make two vertical lines.
The ones digits in the numbers on each blue line are the same: 5s or 0s.
Starting at the top of each red line, the tens digits ascend, while the ones digits descend, e.g. the first line is 3, 12, 21: tens digits (0), 1, 2; ones digits 3, 2, 1.

Page 26
1. a £1.75
   b £1.35
   c £1.44
   d £1.45
   e 28p
   f 76p

2. a £6.51
   b £1.01
   c £2.11
   d £6.31
   e £2.41
   f £1.11
   g £2.61
   h £3.41

Page 27
1. a

obtuse

b

acute

c

acute

d

obtuse

2. a East
   b East
   c South-west
   d East
   e South-east
   f West

Page 28
1. a 07:30
   b 21:00
   c 10:15
   d 16:45
   e 02:10
   f 23:50
   g 9.30 am
   h 3.00 pm
   i 8.15 pm
   j 1.40 pm
   k 10.55 am
   l 10.20 pm

2. a 4 h 15 minutes
   b 3 h 40 minutes
   c 2 h 50 minutes
   d 50 minutes

Page 29
1. a 26
   b Tuesday
   c 17
   d Monday
   e Graph should read 35 books
   f 145

2. Check child's graph

Page 30
1. a £1.80
   b 55 g
   c £5.90
   d 7
   e 10
   f £16.50
   g 240 km
   h 17

2. 150 g margarine
120 g sugar
180 g flour
3 eggs
45 g cocoa powder
60 ml milk

Page 31
1. a C, R, N
   b D (4,9) A (7,6)
     S (2,0)
   c RECTANGLE

2.
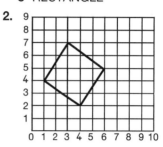

   a The shape is a square.
   b Check the new coordinates for the rectangle.

Page 32
  1. 70
  2. 8000
  3. 600
  4. 90
  5. 6000
  6. 2108
  7. 4090
  8. 7235
  9. 3816
10. 9700

Page 33
  1. 387
  2. 198
  3. 24
  4. 200
  5. 186
  6. £1.56
  7. 8·2 m
  8. 165 ml
  9. £5.33
10. 3.45 m

Page 34
  1. 50 cm
  2. 5 mm
  3. 100 m
  4. 250 ml
  5. 250 g
  6. 38 mm
  7. 52 mm
  8. 63 mm
  9. 26 mm
10. 77 mm

Page 35
  1. 4
  2. 8
  3. 6
  4. 3
  5. 5
  6. pentagon
  7. hexagon
  8. octagon
  9. quadrilateral (trapezium)
10. triangle

Page 36
The missing numbers are in **bold**.
  1. 32 35 38 **41** 44 47 50 53 **56** 59
  2. 48 52 **56** 60 64 68 **72** 76 80 84
  3. 31 29 27 **25** 23 21 **19** 17 15

4. 230 210 **190** 170
150 **130** 110 90 70
5. 76 81 86 91 **96** 101
106 **111** 116
6. –2
7. 4
8. –7
9. –3
10. –1

Page 37
1. 5   6. 5
2. 11   7. 66
3. 24   8. 9
4. 4   9. 12
5. 5   10. 9

Page 38
1. 235p   6. 275p
2. 645p   7. £2.55
3. £3.70   8. £3.15
4. 109p   9. £4.05
5. £2.14   10. £4.10

Page 39
1. $\frac{4}{10} = \frac{2}{5}$
2. $\frac{3}{6} = \frac{1}{2}$
3. $\frac{2}{8} = \frac{1}{4}$
4. $\frac{6}{8} = \frac{3}{4}$
5. $\frac{4}{8} = \frac{1}{2}$
6. $\frac{8}{10}$
7. $\frac{6}{9}$
8. $\frac{1}{4}$
9. $\frac{9}{12}$
10. $\frac{6}{20}$

Page 40
1. 10.25am
2. 6.30pm
3. 11.10pm
4. 6.15am
5. 12.45am
6. 16:30
7. 06:25
8. 17:15
9. 10:20
10. 23:55

Page 41
1. 10
2. 15
3. 11 to 14 people
4. 28 people
5. 62 to 68 people
6. 14
7. 9
8. 5
9. 5
10. 28

Page 42
1. 450
2. 630
3. 810
4. 1070
5. 2340
6. 5.3
7. 47
8. 38
9. 63.5
10. 801

Page 43
1. 178
2. 359
3. 590

4. 838
5. 5639
6. 3085
7. 8863
8. 7700
9. 9184
10. 2131

Page 44
1. £1.92
2. £2.80
3. £2.77
4. £4.13
5. £1.67
6. £2 £2 50p 20p 20p
7. £2 £1 50p
8. £1 10p 2p 1p
9. £2 20p 5p 1p
10. £2 £2 10p 2p 2p

Page 45
1. 105 cm
2. 37 cm
3. 290 cm
4. D
5. A
6. 545 g
7. 1800 km
8. 228 g
9. 85
10. can

Page 46
1. (square-based) pyramid
2. 5 corners
3. 5 faces
4. cylinder
5. 2 edges
6. 3 faces
7. cone
8. 2 faces
9. cuboid
10. 6 faces

Page 47
1. 22   6. 16
2. 30   7. 21
3. 19   8. 26
4. 18   9. 24
5. 36   10. 21

Page 48
1. 95 remainder 3
2. 122 remainder 6
3. 144 remainder 1
4. 71
5. 146 remainder 1
6. 9
7. 8
8. 6
9. 8
10. 7

Page 49
1. £1.10   6. 55p
2. 55p   7. £1.92
3. 80p   8. £3.35
4. 84p   9. £1.43
5. 85p   10. £1.38

Page 50
1. 4·16
2. 14·05
3. 0·24
4. 6·03
5. 9·9
6. 6
7. 2
8. 1

9. 4
10. 4

Page 51
1–5.

6–10.

	even	not even
<10	6	1
not <10	24	13 15

Page 52
1. <
2. <
3. >
4. <
5. >
6. 308 310 318 381
7. 4008 4081 4180 4191
8. 6095 6120 6293 6905
9. 410 2004 2140 4010
10. 902 989 9189 9214

Page 53
1. 496
2. 319
3. 3965
4. 5743
5. 556
6. 1·3
7. 1·5
8. 375
9. 775
10. 450

Page 54
1. 20 squares
2. 28 squares
3. 24 squares
4. 20 squares
5. 18 squares
6. 28 squares
7. 28 cm
8. 22 m
9. 34 cm
10. 54 cm

Page 55

1.

2.

3.

4.

5.

6.

7.

8.

9.

10.

Page 56
Answers 1-3, 4-6, 7-8 and 9-10 can be given in any order.
1. 36   6. 111
2. 110   7. 36
3. 92   8. 92
4. 36   9. 110
5. 99   10. 65

Page 57
1. 42   6. 6
2. 15   7. 20
3. 432   8. 50
4. 42   9. 30
5. 96   10. 9

Page 58
1. 38p
2. £13
3. £2.45
4. 7
5. £4.80
6. £1600
7. £2.80
8. 18p
9. £8.20
10. £2.40

Page 59
1. five
2. one hundredth
3. three tenths
4. twenty
5. nine tenths
6. 0·09
7. 0·45
8. 0·33
9. 0·22
10. 0·05

Page 60
1. 3.45   6. 4.25
2. 7.35   7. 2.30
3. 1.25   8. 5.05
4. 6.30   9. 3.10
5. 10.50   10. 3.30

Page 61
1. 22
2. 24
3. 4
4. 8
5. 3
6. 2
7. weeks 1 and 3
8. 6
9. 105
10. B